A Guide for Using

The Borrowers

in the Classroom

Based on the novel written by Mary Norton

This guide written by **Shelle Allen-Russell**

Teacher Created Materials, Inc.
6421 Industry Way
Westminster, CA 92683
www.teachercreated.com
©1999 Teacher Created Materials, Inc.
Made in U.S.A.
ISBN 1-57690-339-7

Edited by
Mary Kaye Taggart

Illustrated by
Barb Lorseyedi

Cover Art by
Dennis Carmichael

Table of Contents

Introduction

An interesting book can create new ways of viewing life around us. Inside its pages are words and characters which can teach us valuable lessons, challenge creativity, and inspire us to become better people. We can read for enjoyment, knowledge, and guidance. The lives found on the pages of books will impact our lives forever.

In Literature Units great care has been taken to select books that are sure to be great friends. *The Borrowers* is one such book.

Teachers who use this literature unit will find the following features to supplement their own valuable ideas.

- A Sample Lesson Plan
- Pre-reading Activities
- A biographical sketch and picture of the author
- A Book Summary
- Vocabulary Lists and Vocabulary Activity Ideas
- Journal activities
- Chapters grouped for study, with each section including:
  - *quizzes*
  - *hands-on projects*
  - *cooperative learning activities*
  - *cross-curriculum connections*
  - *extension activities to relate to the reader's own life*
- Post-reading Activities
- Book Report Ideas
- Research Ideas
- Culminating Activities
- Three different options for unit tests
- Bibliography
- Answer Key

We are confident that this unit will be a useful addition to your lesson planning. Through the use of our ideas, your students will, we hope, increase the circle of "friends" they can have in books!

Sample Lesson Plan

Each of the lessons suggested below can take from one to several days to complete.

Lesson 1

- Introduce and complete some of the pre-reading activities. (pages 5 and 6)
- Decorate your room with Small Person ID Cards. (page 6)
- Read About the Author with your students. (page 7)
- Introduce the vocabulary words for Section 1. (page 9)

Lesson 2

- Read chapters 1–4. As you read, place the vocabulary words in the context of the story and discuss their meanings. (page 9)
- Do a vocabulary activity. (page 10)
- Make small persons. (page 12)
- Have a debate on borrowing. (page 13)
- Do the Family Classification activity. (page 14)
- Begin Reading Response Journals. (page 15)
- Administer the Section 1 quiz. (page 11)
- Introduce the vocabulary words for Section 2. (page 9)

Lesson 3

- Read chapters 5–8. Place the vocabulary words in the context of the story and discuss their meanings. (page 9)
- Do a vocabulary activity. (page 10)
- Create a home of your own. (page 17)
- Discuss the differences between needs and wants. (page 18)
- Play the I've Been Seen! game. (page 19)
- Design a poster about mercy. (page 20)
- Administer the Section 2 quiz. (page 16)
- Introduce the vocabulary words for Section 3. (page 9)

Lesson 4

- Read chapters 9–12. Place the vocabulary words in the context of the story and discuss their meanings. (page 9)
- Do a vocabulary activity. (page 10)
- Write secret messages. (page 22)
- Send secret messages on a graph. (page 23)
- Find out more about England by doing the English Search. (page 24)

- Choose a pen pal in England or India. (page 25)
- Administer the Section 3 quiz. (page 21)
- Introduce the vocabulary words for Section 4. (page 9)

Lesson 5

- Read chapters 13–16. Place the vocabulary words in the context of the story and discuss their meanings. (page 9)
- Do a vocabulary activity. (page 10)
- Make a classroom quilt. (page 27)
- Map out your own graphed message. (page 28)
- Use borrowing in math. (page 29)
- Make out a will. (page 30)
- Administer the Section 4 quiz. (page 26)
- Introduce the vocabulary words for Section 5. (page 9)

Lesson 6

- Read chapters 17–20. Place the vocabulary words in the context of the story and discuss their meanings. (page 9)
- Do a vocabulary activity. (page 10)
- Create a collage of borrowed items. (page 32)
- Learn about ferrets. (page 33)
- Do telephone math. (page 34)
- Imagine what it would be like to have servants. (page 35)
- Administer the Section 5 quiz. (page 31)

Lesson 7

- Discuss any questions your students may have about the story. (page 36)
- Assign book reports and research projects. (pages 37 and 38)
- Begin working on the culminating activities. (pages 39–42)

Lesson 8

- Administer Unit Tests: 1, 2, and/or 3. (pages 43–45)
- Discuss the test answers and possibilities.
- Discuss the students' reactions to the book.
- Provide a list of related reading for your students. (page 46)

Before the Book

Before you begin reading *The Borrowers* with your students, do some pre-reading activities to stimulate interest and enhance comprehension. Here are some activity assignments which may work well in your class.

1. Design and create word search and/or crossword puzzles, using the vocabulary lists.

2. Predict what the story might be about after studying the cover and reading the title.

3. Discuss borrowing versus stealing. Is there a difference? How are they similar?

4. Collect newspaper articles about theft. On a sheet of poster board measuring 8 ½" x 11" (22 cm x 28 cm), create a collage of the articles. Display your collage on a bulletin board.

5. As a class, brainstorm a list of rules and regulations for borrowing. Write the list on a small chart for each desk.

6. Draw simple comic strip drawings which show a time in your life when you borrowed something that belonged to someone else. The last frame should show the item being returned to its owner.

7. Discuss borrowing in the community, home, and school. As a class, create a chart on the board. Use it to enter data and to respond to the following:

   • What are things in each area which can be borrowed?

   • Name several things under each category which cannot be borrowed for one reason or another.

   • Discuss the reasons to return things which have been borrowed.

   • Discuss and list the consequences for not returning borrowed items.

8. Familiarize yourself with the following English words from England and their definitions.

   • tureen—large soup bowl

   • blotting paper—used to catch ink drips, spills, and blots

   • scullery—room used for washing dishes

   • emigrate—to leave a place

   • bobbles—small balls of fabric (usually on curtains)

   • wainscot—paneling

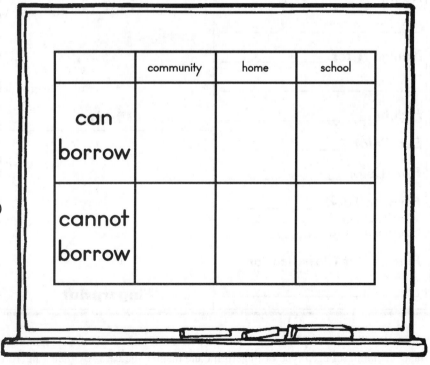

	community	home	school
can borrow			
cannot borrow			

Before the Book *(cont.)*

A Room of Small People!

Imagine waking up this morning as a small person. Your whole world is different; everything is large, and you are miniature. Things are no longer safe for you. You need to find a place to live where you will be safe, where you can keep your belongings, and where you can feel at home.

Your classroom is where you will begin your adventure. Below is a card to be used for identification purposes. Follow the directions carefully to create the "small person" you will become.

First, you will need a new name and information about yourself. You must be no taller than five inches (13 cm). The family in the story had names which were borrowed from things in the human world. Combine several names or borrow a name from something in the large world of the humans to create your own first name. Pick only a first name!

Next, you will need to place a fingerprint on the card below. Ink your left thumb, and place it in the correct location on the card. Look carefully at the types of fingerprints below. Use a magnifying glass to examine your print carefully. Find the pattern which best matches yours. Write its name on the line marked "Fingerprint Classification."

Lastly, draw a picture of your new face in the "photo" part of the card. Use the majority of the space. Draw and color it neatly.

Small Person ID Card

Personal Data

Name _____

_____

Named After _____

_____

Height _____

Eye Color _____

Hair Color _____

Favorite Food _____

Favorite Color _____

Fingerprint Classification

_____

Photo

Fingerprint

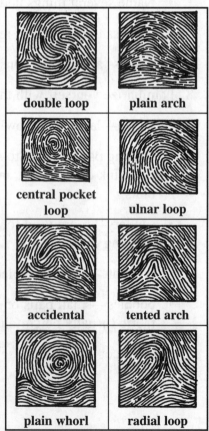

double loop   plain arch

central pocket loop   ulnar loop

accidental   tented arch

plain whorl   radial loop

Note to the Teacher: Collect the completed ID cards and use them to create a bulletin board which looks like a graph. Make a column for each type of fingerprint and display the cards by their fingerprint types. Discuss each pattern.

About the Author

Mary Norton was born on December 10, 1903, in London, England. As a child, she was nearsighted and missed many activities around her. It was at this time that she claimed to have invented the Borrowers. Her childhood home was one much like the one described in her stories.

One day her father, a doctor, bought a large medical practice in the town of Lambeth. There his wealthy patients took advantage of him, neglecting to pay their bills. As a result, when he died, he left her mother virtually penniless with no means to adequately support the children.

Mary Norton was then sent to a Catholic convent school. She hated it and did not do well in her secretarial studies or at her job in a shoemaker's shop. Consequently, she was fired, and when she was fired she began to cry. Her boss kindly asked her, "My child, is there anything else you'd like to do?" She answered, "I love acting."

In 1925 she entered the Old Vic Theater where she began training under many wonderful actors and actresses. This was her favorite time of her life. In 1926 she married Robert Charles Norton. They had four children: Ann, Robert, Guy, and Caroline. For the first few years of their marriage, they lived lavishly in a large home in Portugal. When times became more difficult, they were forced to sell all of their possessions. Her husband then went into the navy.

During the second world war, Mary was sent to America where she had a war job and cared for the children. When she did not have enough time to spend with her children, she quit her job and began writing full time. This allowed her to have more time to spend with her family. After only two years in New York, she returned to England.

After the death of her first husband, she married again in 1970 at the age of 67. She and her second husband lived on the Essex Coast, Ireland, and, finally, England at the time of her death in 1993.

One of her books, *Bed-Knob and Broomstick,* was made into a movie by Disney in 1971. *The Borrowers* was adapted as a record and cassette in 1974 and then served as the basis for a movie in 1998. "The Magic Bed-Knob" and "Bonfires and Broomsticks" were broadcasts by the British Broadcasting Corporation.

Among the books Mary Norton has written are the following:

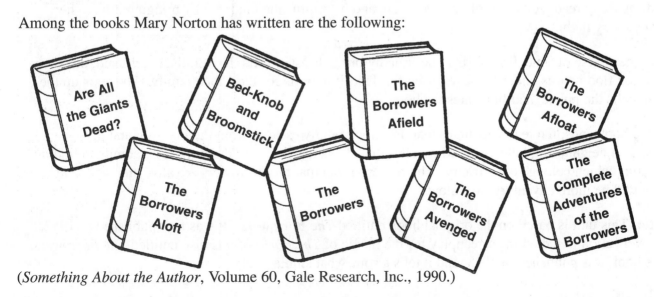

(*Something About the Author*, Volume 60, Gale Research, Inc., 1990.)

The Borrowers

by Mary Norton

(Harcourt Brace Jovanovich, 1952)

(Available in Canada and UK from HBJ; Australia, HBJ Aus.)

The Borrowers takes place in the countryside outside of London, England. A young girl develops a friendship with an elderly woman. The elderly woman, Mrs. May, tells a strange story about a family of "small people" who live under the floor boards of a large, old mansion. There were many families of these little people in generations past, who had lived in the stately home. Now only one family remains, the Clocks—Pod, Homily, and their daughter, Arrietty.

The event that these people fear the most is "being seen" by the humans who live in the home above. Pod and Homily have protected their only child from nearly all of the dangers she could face. Each day they take precautions to shelter her, more for their own selfish reasons than for her actual safety.

Arrietty, on the other hand, is extremely interested in the world outside of her sheltered home. She constantly looks through a grate in the wall and wonders what may be outside in the unknown world. She longs to play with others, and she wants to experience nature firsthand.

One day, a stranger moves into the mansion and disrupts the routine known by the Borrower family. Pod goes "upstairs" to do his usual "borrowing." However, as he begins to come down the curtains, he looks up and notices a boy intently watching his every movement. The boy notices his struggle to descend the curtain without dropping a teacup. He takes the teacup and gently places it on the floor. Also, he reaches up and removes the matching saucer, presenting it to Pod.

Pod is quite shaken when he returns home and suggests that the family emigrate as all of their relatives have done. His wife refuses to leave their lovely home. Arrietty begs to go "upstairs" and learn how to "borrow." She convinces her father that the boy may not intend to hurt them.

Throughout the rest of the book, Arrietty and the boy develop a friendship. She learns that he is visiting from India to recover from an illness, that he has a sister who is bilingual, and that he cannot read. Arrietty reads to him as often as she can, and he returns the kindness by bringing gifts to her family every night.

Over the course of time, his efforts to be friendly bring disaster. Mrs. Driver, the cruel maid, discovers the loose floorboards under the stove, used for depositing gifts for the Clock family. She tears up the floor, calls the police, and fumigates the home.

As the book ends, the reader assumes that the Clock family escapes from the mansion and makes a new home in a neighboring field. Mrs. May states that she is the sister of "the boy." She admits to finding a writing which belonged to Arrietty. The reader knows that the Borrowers are alive and well, and there will be more adventures to follow.

Note: This unit is based on the original book entitled *The Borrowers*. It was first published in 1952. A novelization based on the screenplay for the movie of *The Borrowers* is also entitled *The Borrowers*. This book was published in 1998, and it tells a somewhat similar story.

Vocabulary Lists

The vocabulary words listed below correspond to each section of *The Borrowers*. Ideas for vocabulary activities can be found on page 10 of this book.

Section 1
Chapters 1–4

twilight	particular	fumes	foraged	restlessly
hesitated	exclaim	arrangement	scalding	mechanically
impossible	various	slung	emigrate	dangling

Section 2
Chapters 5–8

obediently	protested	interrupted	accusingly	latched
crouched	breathlessly	stared	trod	steep
skilled	peaky	ponderously	shifted	shrilly

Section 3
Chapters 9–12

fringe	noiselessly	frightened	charming	clatter
enormous	tinkled	impatiently	piercing	half-forgotten
swiftly	courage	thoughtfully	variegated	creaking

Section 4
Chapters 13–16

blindly	fetched	familiar	sharply	disheveled
inspiration	dimly	irritably	drowsily	vigorously
glinted	crumpled	trembling	wavered	envious

Section 5
Chapters 17–20

grunting	deliberate	shuffle	appeased	hastily
jabbering	fearfully	rubbish	genuinely	exposing
fluttering	deflated	moaned	rendered	stench

Vocabulary Activity Ideas

You can help your students learn and retain the vocabulary in *The Borrowers* by providing them with interesting vocabulary activities. Here are some ideas to try.

1. **Word searches and crossword puzzles** are fun for all ages. Students can use the vocabulary words from the story to create puzzles individually or in teams. Have them exchange papers and solve the puzzles. When the papers are completed, the authors can correct them.

2. Encourage the **usage** of vocabulary words! Writing sentences is a very good way to expand usage. Encourage the students to write in themes: silly or ridiculous, vegetables, candy bars, animals, or people. Silly sentences are fun to share with the class!

3. **Vocabulary designs** are always enjoyable and interesting! Have the students select vocabulary words from each chapter. Ask them to lightly draw (in pencil) a design which reminds them of each word. Next, tell them to repeatedly write the vocabulary word around the edge of each shape. They may use any type of medium: colored pencils, markers, crayons, or even paints. This is an excellent activity for use during free time. The end results can be collected and displayed to make an attractive and creative bulletin board.

4. Make **vocabulary games**. Divide the students into groups of three or four. Give each group one piece of poster board that measures 11" x 14" (28 cm x 36 cm). Give them 15 cards, each measuring 3" x 5" (8 cm x 13 cm). Assign each group one section of the vocabulary words. Each group should design a game board, create rules, and make clues for the vocabulary words on their assigned list. Ideas for clue cards may include riddles, sentences with the words left out, or scrambled letters.

5. A **TV news broadcast** is a great way to give the students further experience in using their words. Break the students into groups of three or four. Assign each student a job in the studio: main reporter (one or two), outside reporter, and meteorologist. Have them use the vocabulary words to create "breaking news." Encourage them to use each word in context as often as possible. Have each team present a broadcast to the class. Use a vocabulary list for each group to make sure that they have used each word at least one time.

6. Create **vocabulary comics** on 24" x 6" (61 cm x 15 cm) strips of poster paper. Have the students fold their strips in half, and then in half again, and then in half once more to make eight comic-strip windows per strip. Challenge the students to use 10 vocabulary words in their comic strips. This could be done individually or in groups.

Quiz Time

Answer the following questions about chapters 1–4. If you need more writing space, use the back of this paper or a separate piece of paper.

1. Describe the relationship between Kate and Mrs. May.

   _____

   _____

2. What strange story does Mrs. May begin to tell Kate one day?

   _____

   _____

3. Who told Mrs. May about the Borrowers? How did this person discover them?

   _____

   _____

4. Describe the home of Pod, Homily, and Arrietty Clock.

   _____

   _____

5. What was something Arrietty loved to do regularly? Why was she so careful?

   _____

   _____

6. What is Pod's main occupation? What does Arrietty feel she can do?

   _____

   _____

7. Homily has asked Pod for something special in chapter 3. What is it? Why is she worried?

   _____

   _____

8. Describe each person in the Clock family: Pod, Arrietty, and Homily.

   _____

   _____

9. What scary event occurs for Pod when he retrieves the teacup? What two things does he say must now happen?

   _____

   _____

10. Homily uses what reason to reject Pod's idea of emigration?

   _____

Small Persons Alive!

In this activity you will be using the ID card which you created earlier. Today you will be making an actual model of the tiny person which you have become. Follow the steps below to create your own small person. Try to make it look like the picture you drew on your ID card.

Materials

- 2 chenille sticks
- newspaper cut into ½" x 1" (1.3 x 2.5 cm) strips
- flour
- water
- paintbrushes
- yarn
- tempera paints
- white glue
- scissors
- scraps of felt and other materials
- clear household cement
- any other small items for making clothes or accessories

Directions

1. Make a small loop (like a head shape) in the center of one chenille stick. Twist the chenille stick one time at the base of the loop.

2. Place the second chenille stick through the head loop with half on each side of the loop.

3. Tightly twist the second chenille stick five times to create the torso of your little person.

4. Twist the chenille sticks at the neck three times. Leave equal lengths of excess chenille sticks on each side of the head.

5. Pull the arms out. Make a small, flat loop at the end of each arm, and then fold back and twist three times.

6. Make flat loops at the bottoms of the legs. Fold these back and twist them three times.

7. Bend your figure into the position that you want him or her to be in permanently.

8. Mix a paste out of flour and water in a small tray. The mixture should be the consistency of a thick glue.

9. Dip strips of newspaper into the paste and wrap all parts of the body and head with several layers. Make sure that none of the chenille stick can be seen. Allow the figure to dry.

10. Paint your small person any skin color. Let it dry.

11. Cut pieces of yarn for the hair and glue it on. Add facial features with a fine marker.

12. After your person is complete, design clothes out of material. Glue the clothes onto the body.

Note to the Teacher: You may choose to spray-paint the skin-colored paint on the figures for the students. The next day the students can dress and put the finishing touches on their figures.

Debate: To Borrow or Not to Borrow?

In this exercise you are going to get some feedback from other people in your class on your writing. You will also share and debate your ideas with others.

On a plain sheet of paper, take 15 minutes to make a first draft on one of the following topics related to *The Borrowers*. Give your writing piece a catchy title.

- Define borrowing. Is it a good thing or a bad thing? State at least three reasons to support your answer.
- Are family and relatives important to you? Why or why not? If so, what traditions have you started to build together as a family? If not, what kinds of things do you think should take place in groups that feel family is very important?
- What are some things parents try to shield or protect their children from? Can parents go too far in making rules and guidelines? Can children go too far in defying parents' rules? State examples.

When you have finished writing, break into groups of three. Pass your paper to the person on your left. Take a paper from the person on your right. Read each draft and discuss your feelings versus the writer's feelings.

Next, form debate teams. Debate one of the above issues in front of the class. Make sure both sides have some persuasive arguments. (**Note:** You may wish to videotape the debates in place of live debates.)

After the debates have been completed, take a class survey to find out how most people sided on the subjects. Chart the survey results on a chart on the chalkboard.

The debates may be made to look professional by seating students dressed in businesslike attire behind a rectangular table and/or setting up a stage (like on a talk show).

	Borrowing	Families and Traditions	Rules and Guidelines
Side A	‖‖ ‖ ‖	‖‖ ‖‖ ‖‖ ‖	‖‖ ‖‖
Side B	‖‖ ‖‖ ‖ ‖	‖ ‖ ‖ ‖	‖‖ ‖‖

Family Classification

In *The Borrowers* all of the "small people" belong to a family group. Pod, Homily, and Arrietty make up the Clock family. They have this last name because their home is under the clock in the mansion. In order to go "borrowing" or to "leave" the home, they use the small hole under the clock in the hallway.

Look at your classroom graph bulletin board which identifies the different people in each fingerprint pattern group. This group will be your "family" for this activity.

Note to the Teacher: The groups may be combined if there are only one or two students in a fingerprint pattern category.

Part 1

Your family (all of those in the same pattern category as you) will need to have a name. You will need to choose a name from the classroom. As a group, decide the last name of your family and where you will live (in the classroom). Remember, the Clock family (Pod, Homily, and Arrietty) were the only ones who lived under the home. The rest of the Borrowers lived in the home in different locations.

Write the name of your family, the names of the members, where you will live, and why you chose that area of the classroom in the spaces below. When you have completed both parts of this lesson, share the information below with the class, and turn it (or a copy of it) in to your teacher for his or her records.

Part 2

Now that your group has a name, create some things that will be unique to your family. Create two traditions (for example, most people eat turkey for Thanksgiving) and two customs (for example, we shake hands when we greet each other). Fill in the spaces below with your ideas after your group has discussed each one thoroughly. The ideas written down should be agreed upon by the majority of the group. (Remember, you are a Borrower and your ideas must reflect this.)

Examples

Human Tradition: eat turkey for Thanksgiving
New Borrower Tradition: eat scalloped carrots and burgers for Franksgiving

Human Custom: shake hands when greeting each other
New Borrower Custom: wiggle ears and knock knees when greeting each other

Family Last Name _____

We live _____

We live here because_____

_____

First Name of Each Member _____

_____

Traditions _____

_____

Customs _____

_____

Reading Response Journals

One great way to ensure that the reading of *The Borrowers* becomes a personal experience for each student is to include the use of reading response journals in your plans. In these journals students can be encouraged to respond to the story in a number of ways. Since Arrietty keeps a concise journal throughout the entire story, this theme fits in perfectly with reading response journals.

Suggestions for Using Reading Response Journals

- Tell the students that the purpose of their journals is to record their thoughts, ideas, observations, and questions as they read *The Borrowers.*

- Provide the students with (or ask them to suggest) topics from the story that would stimulate writing. Here are some examples from the chapters in Section 1.

  —List some of the benefits and concerns of a person who is very small. Describe both.

  —Some call the Borrowers selfish and conceited. What does this mean, and what is your opinion of the Borrowers?

  —Being an only child can sometimes be very lonely. What are some of the advantages to being an only child? What are some of the disadvantages?

- Ask the students to draw their responses to certain events or characters in the story.

- Tell the students to use their journals to record diary responses on a regular basis, just as Arrietty did.

- Encourage the students to bring their journal entries to life! Ideas generated from their journal writing can be used to create plays, debates, songs, puppet shows, displays, cartoon strips, and stories.

- Give the students quotes from the novel and ask them to write their own responses. (Make sure that you do this before you go over the quotations in class.) In groups, they could list different responses to the same quote.

Allow your students time to write in their journals daily. Personal reflections can be read by the teacher, but no corrections or letter grades should be assigned. Credit should be given for effort, and all of the students who sincerely try should be awarded credit. If a grade is desired, grade according to the number of entries completed.

Quiz Time

Answer the following questions about chapters 5–8. If you need more writing space, use the back of this paper or a separate piece of paper.

1. On the back of this paper, write a one-paragraph summary of the major events that happen in chapters 5–8. Then complete the rest of the questions on this page.

2. Why does Homily feel she is largely to blame for Pod being "seen"? What may occur as a result of being "seen"?

   _____

   _____

3. What reason does Homily give to explain the fact that their family has been able to survive in this home while all of the rest of the families have had to move out?

   _____

   _____

4. Who sees Pod? What does this person do to assist him?

   _____

5. Why do Arrietty's parents wake her up?

   _____

   _____

6. Pod and Homily feel good about the environment they have created for their daughter. How does Arrietty feel about their living arrangements? Cite some supporting examples from the story.

   _____

   _____

7. How does Arrietty feel about emigrating? Why does Homily suggest Arrietty borrow?

   _____

   _____

8. Have you ever wanted to borrow something? What was it? Did you return it?

   _____

   _____

9. Why is Arrietty so good at the beginning of chapter 7? What special things does she do?

   _____

   _____

10. When Arrietty first goes upstairs, describe what happens.

   _____

   _____

A Home All Your Own

A large part of *The Borrowers* takes place in the home underneath the clock. The Clock family (Homily in particular) has gone to great pains to decorate the home and to create a warm atmosphere.

You will now have the opportunity to create your own home in a shoebox. Decorate it as you would if you were a Borrower.

Gather the following supplies for your shoebox home. Be sure to ask your parents, siblings, or any others for their permission before you borrow objects from them to use in your project.

Materials

- one shoebox
- scraps of used notebook paper (for wallpaper)
- stamps (used)
- empty thread spools
- thimbles (plastic or metal)
- any other small objects

Sketch your decorating plans below before actually creating them.

Note to the Teacher: These projects may be displayed around the room, in the school office, or in the school library.

Want or Need?

In *The Borrowers* the Clock family lives underneath a large grandfather clock. While the Clocks' home seems especially unusual to us, all homes are different. No home has exactly the same things in it because each family likes, believes in, and collects different things. Some items are things that we need to survive, some are for comfort, and some are just plain frivolous.

With a partner, discuss and fill in the chart below. After you have completed it, discuss it with the rest of the class. Some examples have been done for you.

Table of Needs, Wants, and Luxuries			
Needs	**Wants**	**Luxuries**	**Reasons**
clothing			keep warm, health
	microwave		cooks food quickly
		sports car	great to ride in!

I've Been Seen!

This is an exciting game which can be played inside or outside the classroom. Explain the game carefully before playing.

Materials

- poster-board strips which are 2" x 5" (5 cm x 13 cm)
- string
- a single hole puncher
- three colors of markers

Before the Game

1. Punch single holes in the centers of the ends of the poster-board strips.

2. Write random three-to-four-digit numbers on each piece of poster board. Do these in three sets of 10. Use a different color of marker for each set.

3. Tie one piece of string in each end of the poster-board strips.

4. Divide the students into groups of 10 (or as close to 10 as possible).

Object of the Game

Catch and collect as many numbers from other teams as possible. The team with the most cards is the winner.

Game Directions

Give each group of 10 students one set of poster-board numbers. Have the students tie the poster-board number cards to their heads like headbands, while protecting their numbers from being seen by the other teams. When you give a signal to go, the students may move freely around the room (or on the playground). However, they must try to shield their numbers from being seen by the other teams. Allow each team to have a home base where it starts, but each team must leave its base and wander freely when you give the signal. A team member must give up his or her number if another team is able to identify it correctly. The students who lose their numbers must return to their home base and wait out the remainder of the game. Allow about 10 minutes for each game, then blow a whistle, redistribute the numbers, and play again.

Mission of Mercy

Throughout *The Borrowers,* several of the characters help when they do not have to become involved. At the end of the fourth chapter, the boy helps Pod Clock as he struggles to climb down from the curtain with a teacup.

People can always use a helping hand. We can make our world a better place by looking for ways to help others, even if they do not ask. Most of the time, the person being helped is very grateful for the assistance.

Part 1

Break into groups of two or three people. Bring newspapers or magazines from home. Search these materials for articles about people in our society who are lending a helping hand to others in need. Cut out the articles that most interest you. Paste the articles onto a piece of 11" x 14" (30 cm x 36 cm) poster board. Cover the entire poster board with articles and pictures which show people helping others. After your poster is done, share the article that your group finds to be the most interesting with the rest of the class. Display your poster in your classroom.

Part 2

In your same group, design a "Ways to Impact Our World" poster. On the poster give suggestions for helping others, draw diagrams or pictures, or add anything else which might encourage others to get involved in helping without expecting something in return. Ask for permission to post your poster in a visible place around your school campus.

Part 3

If the students in your class are interested, form a club which meets at lunch or at a designated time each week. Choose a name for your club. Look for ways to help others at your school, home, in your community, or anywhere. Keep a log of the activities that you help with, the person or people helped, and the reactions of the individual(s) being helped. Use the log as a way to encourage each other to believe that you are impacting your corner of the world in a positive way!

Quiz Time

Answer the following questions about chapters 9–12. If you need more writing space, use the back of this paper or a separate piece of paper.

1. On the back of this page, write a one-paragraph summary of the major events that happen in chapters 9–12. Then complete the rest of the questions on this page.

2. In Chapter 8 Pod lets Arrietty out of his sight to go somewhere. Where does she go? What does Homily tell her?

   _____

3. Arrietty is so fascinated with the outdoors that she forgets to be cautious. What occurs?

   _____

   _____

4. In her conversation with the boy, how does Arrietty see the world?

   _____

   _____

5. What adventures did Pod's uncle have in the stockpot?

   _____

   _____

6. What do you think Arrietty means when she says that Borrowers only need a few humans "to keep us"? (the end of chapter 9)

   _____

   _____

7. When Pod talks to Great-Aunt Sophy, where does she think he comes from? What does she think he is? _____

   _____

8. Great-Aunt Sophy is very different in the morning. How does the boy describe her? What does she make him do each morning?

   _____

   _____

9. Arrietty almost gives her knowledge of the boy away in chapter 11. What does she say?

   _____

   _____

10. What two things does Arrietty do without her parents' knowledge or consent?

   _____

   _____

The Secret Message!

Arrietty planned to leave a note for the boy under a mat in the hall. It was not in code but that might have been a good idea. Pretend Arrietty did write her letter in a code. Her code might look like the one below.

Part 1

Get together with those who are in your family group and use the code below to find out Arrietty's secret message.

2	7	3	1	9	4	5	8	0	6	&	@	#	:	!	)	(	_	^	%	$	=	/	?	>	,
a	b	c	d	e	f	g	h	i	j	k	l	m	n	o	p	q	r	s	t	u	v	w	x	y	z

Pretend that you are now a very small person, no taller than six inches (15 cm).

——— ——— — — ———
:!/   %82%   0   2#   ^#2@@

——— ——————— ——— ——— ———!
8!/   10449_9:%   %89   /!_@1   @!!&^

Part 2

After you have finished Part 1, create a code for your family group to use. Fill in the blocks for each letter of the alphabet with the new code. Make sure that each family member has a copy of the code, and give a copy to your teacher. Create several messages for others in your family. Make sure to write them from the person you have become to the person he or she has become. Write your messages on small pieces of paper! Leave them in pre-arranged places in the classroom.

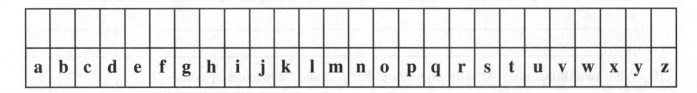

a	b	c	d	e	f	g	h	i	j	k	l	m	n	o	p	q	r	s	t	u	v	w	x	y	z

Mapping Out My Message (Part 1)

Arrietty and the boy could have used any kind of coded message. Below is a sample of a different type of code. This one uses a grid as a message board. The layout is of a classroom. Use the grid coordinates to find out what the message reads.

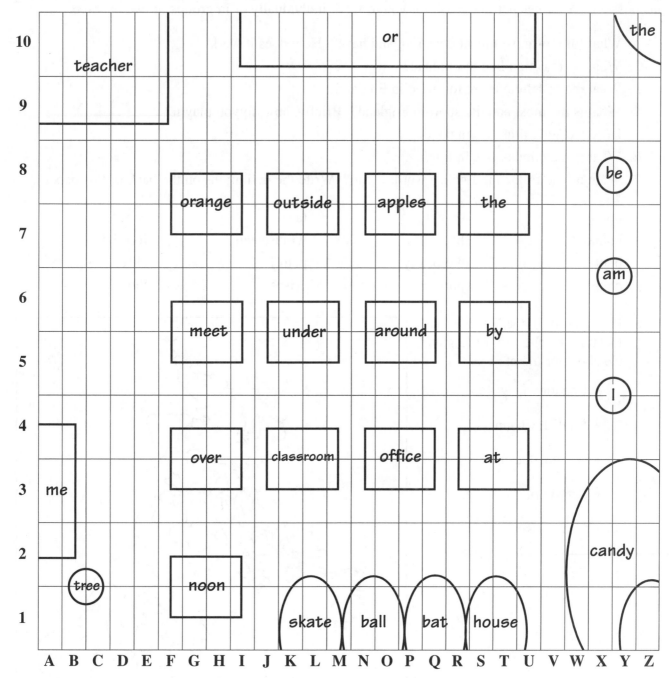

Decode the secret message below by looking up the given coordinates on the grid.

G-6	A-3	M-7	Z-10	L-3	S-5	U-7	B-1	T-3	G-2

English Search

The story of *The Borrowers* takes place on the outskirts of London, England. Use encyclopedias, books about England, and any other useful resources to find the answers to the questions below. Write your answers for questions 1–6 on a separate piece of paper and make all of your answers as complete as possible. Your teacher may wish for you to work individually or in groups of two or three.

1. What form of government does England have? How does it work?

2. What is education like in England?

3. What major religions are followed in England?

4. What is the most popular sport in England? Briefly, how do you play it?

5. Describe agriculture in England.

6. What is the climate like in England?

7. What do the following English words mean? Write the definitions on the back of this paper.

bobby	draughts	ta	cooker
bonnet	lift	windscreen	fortnight
boot	motorway	petrol	cheers
chips	jumper	crisps	loo

8. Find and fill in the listed locations on the map of England. Neatly color the map.

- London

- English Channel

- Atlantic Ocean

- Liverpool

- Cambridge

- Chester

- Bristol

- Plymouth

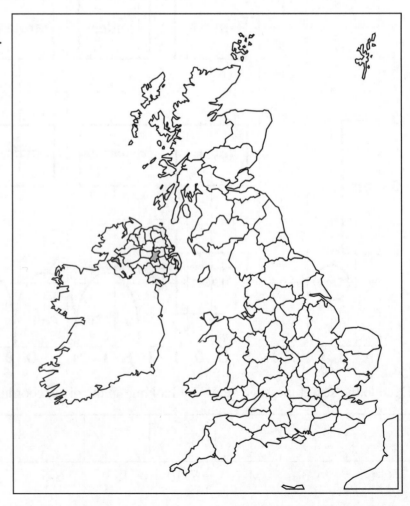

Pen Pals in England or India

Arrietty sent a letter to an uncle (and his family) she had never met. She wished to find out about their lives and to see if they were still doing well. She was curious and inquisitive. Are you ever curious about the lives of people who live in other places?

Even today, life in the United States is quite different from life in the English countryside. Both places may speak the same language, but many words, customs, foods, and traditions are very different from each other.

In India they do not speak English as their primary language, and life is even more different than life in England.

In order to understand life better in both England and India, we can do many different things. We can read books, watch movies, and develop friendships. However, the best way is by learning about or interacting with actual people of these countries. Below are two agencies which you can use to help you find pen pals in England and/or India. Be sure to tell the organization that you contact which country, England or India, you wish to communicate with and include your full name and address.

Ask your pen pal as many questions as you can think of about his or her country. Share the information that you discover with your friends and teacher. Send pictures of yourself and of where you live. Ask your pen pal to send pictures to you as well.

Note to the Teacher: You may wish to make a bulletin board out of the letters, pictures, and information that your students receive.

Quiz Time

Answer the following questions about chapters 13–16. If you need more writing space, use the back of this paper or a separate piece of paper.

1. On the back of this paper, write a one-paragraph summary of the major events that happen in chapters 13–16. Then complete the rest of the questions on this page.

2. In chapter 13, Arrietty begins acting strangely. What is she worried about? What lie does she tell to her mother?

    _____

    _____

3. When Arrietty realizes that the gates are open, where does she go?

    _____

4. Why does the boy not get mad at Arrietty when she explains why she had not read to him?

    _____

    _____

5. What special thing does the boy have for Arrietty?

    _____

6. What does Uncle Hendreary ask Arrietty to do?

    _____

    _____

7. Pod discovers Arrietty upstairs. Describe what happens.

    _____

    _____

    _____

8. What are Homily and Pod really concerned about? How does Pod feel about "human beans"?

    _____

    _____

9. What does the boy do which frightens Homily tremendously?

    _____

    _____

10. What does the boy give to the Clocks which brings great joy to Homily? How does Pod have to deal with it?

    _____

    _____

Borrowers' Quilt

Have your class make a quilt based on *The Borrowers*. To make this quilt each person starts with an 8 ½" x 8 ½" (22 cm x 22 cm) square of white paper. Each square will represent an event, object, or thing which reminds the artist of any part of the book. The designs may be created by drawing, painting, or using ripped, torn, or cut paper shapes and glue.

Assign a group of students to design quilt squares for each section of the book. You may wish to do this as an ongoing activity throughout the unit so that you can include the entire book, beginning to end. Use the following sign-up sheet to evenly distribute the number of students creating blocks for each section. Include due dates for the blocks. These dates may be different for each section, depending on how your reading of *The Borrowers* is progressing.

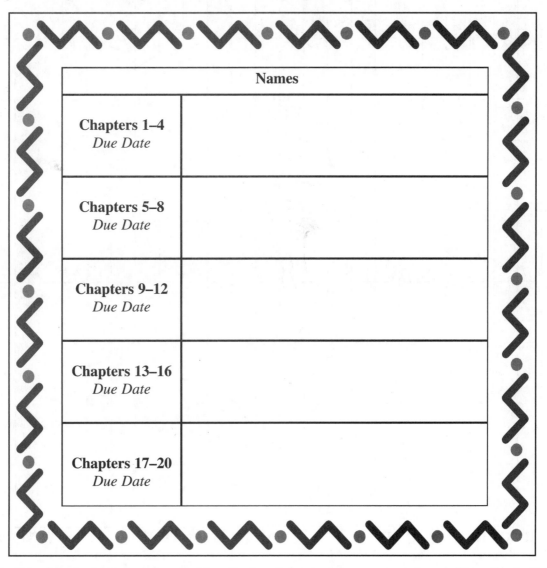

	Names
Chapters 1–4 *Due Date*	
Chapters 5–8 *Due Date*	
Chapters 9–12 *Due Date*	
Chapters 13–16 *Due Date*	
Chapters 17–20 *Due Date*	

When all of the blocks have been turned in, display them together as an entire quilt on the bulletin board. Discuss the finished quilt and its squares.

Variation: You may wish to use squares of actual material for the blocks. The students can use fabric scraps and fabric glue to create their designs. A parent volunteer may then be willing to sew the blocks together on a sewing machine.

Mapping Out My Message (Part 2)

In the last section you decoded a message that was based on a code that used a classroom floor plan (page 23). Now it is your turn to take charge. On the grid below draw 10 simple objects in your classroom. Decide on a message that is 10 words or less. Write the words from your message and some extra random words on the objects. Make a message for a friend or another family group by placing the coordinates of the words under the blank boxes.

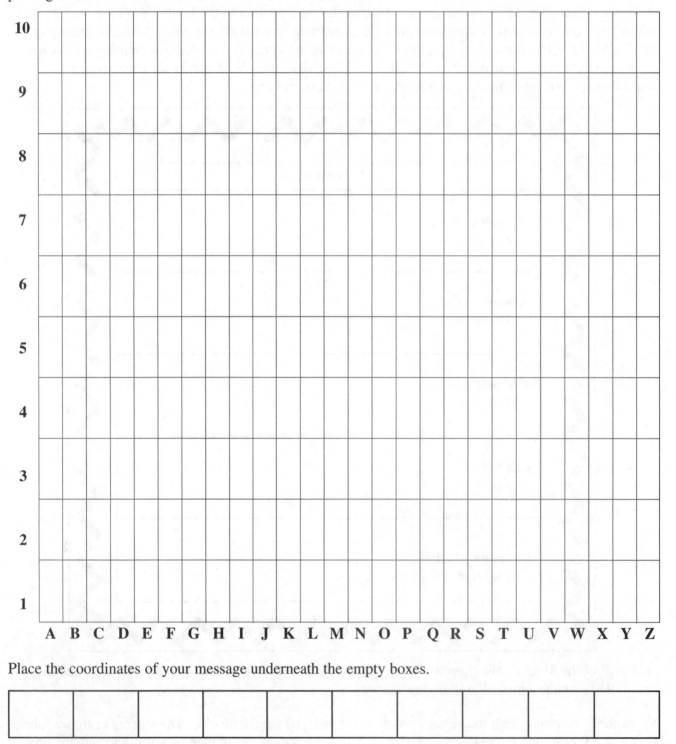

Place the coordinates of your message underneath the empty boxes.

Borrowing in the Mansion

In the story of *The Borrowers*, the borrowing that the Clock family does starts to get out of control. They start to borrow out of greed rather than for survival. In our lives we sometimes borrow things from other people, but (hopefully) we do not do it often, and we always return the items.

In mathematics it is perfectly acceptable to borrow when we are subtracting. There is nothing questionable about it, and it must be done in order to let us know how much we will have left over in the end.

In this activity pretend that dear Aunt Sophy wishes to give her old mansion to the person who is the best at borrowing. Some of the windows have math problems. Start with number one and complete the problems in order. See how successfully you can borrow your way through the mansion. When your work is complete, ask your teacher for the answers, and check your work. See the bottom of the page to find out where you stand in Aunt Sophy's will.

10.
$$467 - 289$$

9.
$$3956 - 989$$

8.
$$8578 - 924$$

7.
$$902 - 693$$

6.
$$91 - 18$$

5.
$$347 - 259$$

4.
$$545 - 368$$

3.
$$6592 - 4875$$

2.
$$8611 - 3579$$

1.
$$86 - 79$$

Aunt Sophy's Will

10 correct: You inherit the mansion.

8–9 correct: You inherit the servants and her model car.

7 correct: You inherit her jewelry.

6 or fewer correct: You get to work for the new owner.

Making Out My Will

When Aunt Sophy dies, she is sure to leave a will and share her possessions with her loved ones. A will is a written document which tells who will receive a person's belongings after he or she dies. Wills are usually written after a great deal of thought and consideration.

Make a will for the little person you created earlier in this unit. List silly things that the little person could give away to the others in your family group or another family group in your classroom.

Example: I, Butter Jo Refrigerator, being of sound mind and body on this 14th day of May 2000, leave my possessions to the people listed below.

I will my favorite doll, Matilda, to my dear sister, Pudding Pop.

I will my teddy bear, Buttercup, to my little brother, French Fry.

I, _____, being of sound mind and body on this

_____ (date) day of _____ (month)

_____ (year), leave my possessions to the people listed below.

I will my _____ to _____.

I will my _____ to _____.

I will my _____ to _____.

I will my _____ to _____.

I will my _____ to _____.

I will my _____ to _____.

Signature _____

Note to the Teacher: When the students are finished with the wills, allow them to share them with each other, display them on a bulletin board, or collect them in a classroom binder.

Quiz Time

Answer the following questions about chapters 17–20. If you need more writing space, use the back of this paper or a separate piece of paper.

1. On the back of this paper, write a one-paragraph summary of the major events that happen in chapters 17–20 and then complete the following questions.

2. How has life changed for the Clock family since they met the boy?

   _____

   _____

   _____

3. Who in the big house begins to notice that things are missing?

   _____

4. How do the Clocks feel about their sudden wealth? Why are they sad?

   _____

   _____

5. What do Arrietty's parents now allow her to do that was forbidden before?

   _____

   _____

6. What does Mrs. Driver discover under the floorboards? What else does she think she saw?

   _____

   _____

   _____

7. How does the boy try to help the Clock family? What does Mrs. Driver do to him?

   _____

   _____

   _____

8. Mrs. Driver accuses the boy of thievery. How does he explain the missing items?

   _____

   _____

9. What terrible thing happens next?

   _____

   _____

10. What does Mrs. May own that once belonged to Arrietty?

   _____

Borrowing and the Borrowers' Collage

Part 1: Borrowing

Pretend that you and your classmates are Borrowers. Over the next 24 hours try to "borrow" as many of the following items as possible. Also, try to gather more than one of some of the items. You can do your borrowing individually or in your family group. Gather your items in a plastic bag or a bag with a twist tie.

Just like a real Borrower, you will not be returning these items when the activity is over so be sure to ask for permission before taking anything which is not yours. Check off the items that you borrow.

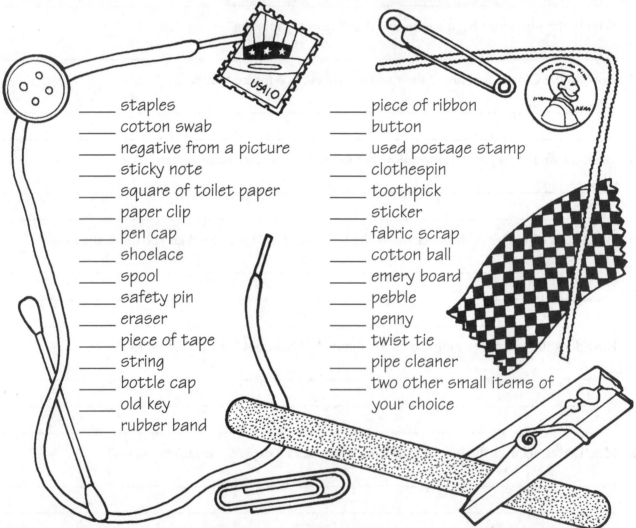

_____ staples
_____ cotton swab
_____ negative from a picture
_____ sticky note
_____ square of toilet paper
_____ paper clip
_____ pen cap
_____ shoelace
_____ spool
_____ safety pin
_____ eraser
_____ piece of tape
_____ string
_____ bottle cap
_____ old key
_____ rubber band

_____ piece of ribbon
_____ button
_____ used postage stamp
_____ clothespin
_____ toothpick
_____ sticker
_____ fabric scrap
_____ cotton ball
_____ emery board
_____ pebble
_____ penny
_____ twist tie
_____ pipe cleaner
_____ two other small items of your choice

Part 2: The Borrowers' Collage

After you have borrowed as many items as you can find, glue them onto an 8 ½" x 11" (22 cm x 28 cm) sheet of colored construction paper or poster board. Create interesting designs with the items and title your final product.

Note to the Teacher: You may wish to turn Part 1 of this activity into a contest similar to a scavenger hunt. Offer a prize to the individual or family group with the most objects. Also, if there is enough classroom space, display the finished collages in a corner of the room.

Discover the Ferret

Mrs. Driver and Mr. Crampfurl were sure that the boy had a ferret. They discussed it several times. They had varying opinions about it, but they were convinced he had a pet of some kind. Below you can find out more about this interesting and unusual animal.

Part 1

In your family group, read the information below about the ferret. Discuss the questions with the others in your group. Write the answers for the entire group on one sheet of paper.

The black-footed ferret is the largest true weasel. It can grow up to 18 inches (46 cm) in length. Its tail may grow as long as six inches (15 cm). Female ferrets are generally smaller than the males. Ferrets' coats are yellowish in color, and they have black bands around their eyes. A ferret has black feet and legs and a black-tipped tail. It lives in burrows under the ground and hunts by using scent and sound. Ferrets which have been domesticated are the same shape and length as the wild ones but can weigh as much as five pounds (2.3 kg). They are often found in hutches in the backyards of cottages in rural England. Ferrets are almost never found in the homes of nobility.

Ferrets have been mentioned throughout history. During the 14th century, licenses were granted by King Richard II of England to use the ferret as an animal for hunting rabbits (but he forbid their use on Sundays). Aristotle of Greece seemed to mention ferrets in 350 B.C., Genghis Khan might have had an albino ferret as a pet in the 13th century, and Isodore de Seville of Europe refers to an animal (probably a ferret) in 600 A.D. which was brought to England by the Romans or Normans.

The black-footed ferret is originally from North America. This ferret used to live on the American prairies; however, today it is considered an endangered species. Not much information is known about ferrets, and it is feared they may become extinct before enough data can be gathered.

Questions:

1. Describe the physical characteristics of a ferret.

2. Why do you think we do not know much about ferrets?

3. When has the ferret been mentioned in history?

4. Discuss the similarities and differences between the black-footed ferret and the domesticated ferret.

Part 2

Use the facts that you have learned about the ferret to create a game. The game should somehow reinforce the knowledge you have gained. Make sure to include game cards, rules, a game board, and the object of the game.

Phone the Police

The Borrowers frightened Mrs.Driver so much that she was insistent on calling in the authorities to help with the problem. She wanted them eliminated immediately so that life could return to its normal, slow, predictable ways.

Each problem below is written in a phone code. You can find the numbers by using the telephone as your guide. For example, A stands for the number 2. Write and solve the problems on the back of this paper. Show your answers in the boxes below. After you have completed the problems, check your work, and see how you "add up" according to Mrs. Driver's scorecard.

Be sure to align the columns of numbers correctly before you add them up.

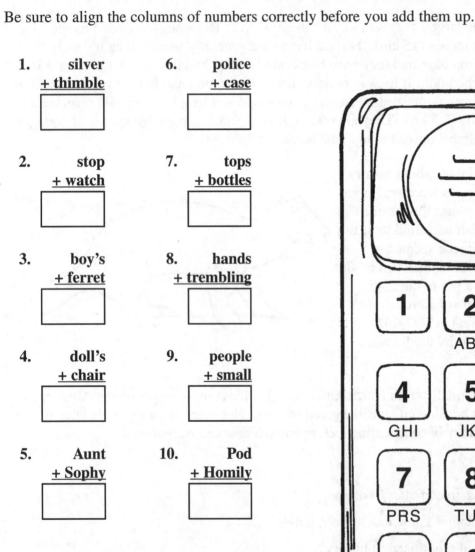

1.   silver
     + thimble

2.   stop
     + watch

3.   boy's
     + ferret

4.   doll's
     + chair

5.   Aunt
     + Sophy

6.   police
     + case

7.   tops
     + bottles

8.   hands
     + trembling

9.   people
     + small

10.   Pod
     + Homily

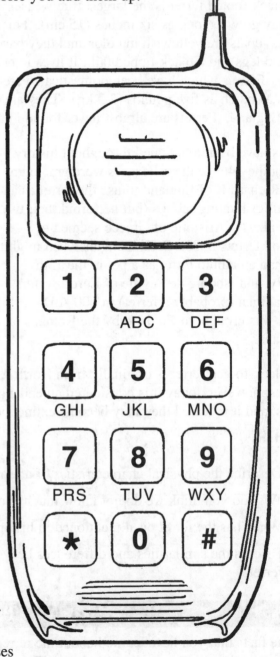

Mrs. Driver's Scorecard

- 10 points = High tea—you can borrow the car.
- 8–9 points = Regular tea—and you get a scone.
- 7 = You get a cup of tea.
- 6 or less = She does not trust you, and she chases
you off with her slipper.

A Cook and a Gardener

The little boy in *The Borrowers* is staying in a mansion near London, England. The mansion has a cook and a gardener. Imagine having a cook and a gardener who lived with you at all times. Life would probably be a lot different. Answer the following questions. If you need more writing space, use the back of this paper or another piece of paper.

1. What would be the best part about having a cook who lives with you? What would be the worst part?

   _____

   _____

2. A gardener is responsible for taking care of the landscape, gardening, and yard. What things might you most like to have him show you about his job?

   _____

   _____

3. What would it be like to have someone live with you at all times? Would it ever become bothersome? Why?

   _____

   _____

4. Describe the cook, Mrs. Driver, in the story. Consider her personality, actions, and daily behavior.

   _____

   _____

5. Describe Mr. Crampfurl, the gardener. Tell how we know that he was very curious about what the boy was looking for.

   _____

   _____

6. If you could have a cook fix any food for you, what would you eat? Plan all three meals for four days. Make sure to include snacks.

	Day 1	Day 2	Day 3	Day 4
breakfast				
lunch				
dinner				
snacks				

Any Questions?

When you finished reading *The Borrowers*, did you have any questions that were left unanswered? Write your questions here.

_____

_____

_____

_____

_____

Next, get into your family group of little people, and discuss the following questions. When you are done, discuss your group's answers with the rest of your class.

- How did Homily's greed interfere with her relationships with Pod and Arrietty?

- How was Arrietty's thinking different from that of her parents?

- Why do you think that the little boy became so involved with the Clock family?

- What do you think life was like for the little boy in that big house? Give examples.

- How important is family to Pod? Homily? Arrietty?

- How does Arrietty's opinion of emigrating differ from her parents' opinions? Why?

- What does Arrietty not understand about the world outside of her grate?

- What kind of person is Mrs. Driver? Give examples to support your answer.

- Why do you think Great-Aunt Sophy spends every afternoon and evening drinking?

- Is borrowing really wrong? What are some basic rules for borrowing?

- Is there a difference between borrowing and stealing?

- If you borrow something and forget to return it, is it really stealing? Why or why not?

- Did the boy lose his perspective on borrowing as he took more and more to the Clocks?

Book Report Ideas

There are many ways to report on a book once you have read it. After you have finished reading *The Borrowers*, choose one method of reporting on the book. It may be a way your teacher suggests, an idea of your own, or one of the ways mentioned below.

Book Character

This report requires some creativity and imagination. Choose one character in the book: the boy, one of the Clocks, Mrs. Driver, Mr. Crampfurl, or Great-Aunt Sophy. Dress up as the character. Tell the story from this character's perspective in front of your class.

Canned Report

This report is dispensed from a cardboard cylinder of some type (like an oatmeal container). Take several sheets of paper and glue them together end to end. Fold them in half the long, thin way. Cut the strips in half and glue the ends of the long strips together. After the glue has dried, divide it into frames, using a pencil. Draw cartoon pictures about the story in the frames. Slit the cardboard container lengthwise. Roll up your story and insert it in the cylinder. Pull the story slowly through the slit. When you are done, roll up the story strip, and put it in the cylinder so that it will be ready to show again.

Invisible Report

This report is done with lemon juice and a toothpick. Dip the toothpick in lemon juice repeatedly, and use it as a pencil. Write the title of the book and a two-paragraph summary on a sheet of white paper. Let the paper dry and hand it in to your teacher. Be sure to include your name. Your teacher will read your report by holding it up to a light source.

Police Report

This is a report of just the facts. If you think that you might someday want to be a police officer, this report style is for you. Write a one-page report on the book from the perspective of a police officer. When police officers arrive at a crime scene, they try to gather the facts (the who, what, when, where, why, and how) of the story. They are not usually interested in opinions or embellishments. Present your factual book report to the class.

Great-Aunt Sophy's Memory Trunk

Create a small trunk out of a shoebox and decorate it. Put at least seven things inside that remind you of events in the story. Bring the trunk to school, and share your memories of *The Borrowers* as you show each item.

Who's Who?

This report concentrates on describing the characters of the story. Make an eight-page booklet. Devote one page to each of the following characters: Great-Aunt Sophy, Mrs. May, the boy, Mrs. Driver, Mr. Crampfurl, Homily, Pod, and Arrietty. Write one paragraph describing each person; write a second paragraph about his or her role in the story and then draw a small portrait.

Research Ideas

Describe three things that you read about in *The Borrowers* that you would like to learn more about.

1. _____

   _____

2. _____

   _____

3. _____

   _____

Work individually or in a group to research one or more of the areas that you named above or one of the areas that are listed below. Share your findings with the rest of the class in an oral presentation.

- **London, England**
  - -foods
  - -customs
  - -history
  - -weather
  - -geography

- **The Weasel Family** (*give a brief summary and a family tree*)
  - -ferrets
  - -skunks
  - -weasels
  - -minks
  - -polecats

- **India**
  - -foods
  - -customs
  - -history
  - -weather
  - -geography

- **Rheumatic Fever**
  - -what it is
  - -how to treat it
  - -symptoms

- **Famous English People Who Have Influenced Our World**

  1. **Lady Diana Spencer**
     - -childhood
     - -adult life
     - -accomplishments

  2. **The Beatles**
     - -who they were
     - -what they did
     - -a short summary about each member

  3. **Winston Churchill**
     - -childhood
     - -adult life
     - -accomplishments

  4. **Queen Victoria**
     - -childhood
     - -adult life
     - -accomplishments

Classroom Teatime

Throughout *The Borrowers*, the characters often mention teatime. England is a country steeped in traditions and rituals. Teatimes are not as commonly observed today, but they are still part of the culture. In order to understand the teatime ritual, it may help to experience one in your own classroom. Celebrate your teatime with the students' parents, grandparents, or with elderly people at a nursing home or care center.

In England, high tea was a formal occasion. Men and women used to dress very formally to celebrate. Behavior at these occasions was almost stiff and formal. Manners were strictly observed. It was a social occasion as well as a meal.

To create a tea for your classroom, break the students into groups. You may wish to modify some of the following directions to fit your classroom needs; they are simply meant to be general guidelines.

- **Food Committee**—It is the responsibility of this committee to plan the food and bring paper serving dishes. Silver-colored plastic or paper dishes can be purchased at some grocery or discount stores for relatively little. The recipes on pages 40 and 41 are authentic English tea foods. This committee is also in charge of planning the drinks . . . especially the tea!

- **Decorations Committee**—The decorations committee will plan the table decor, including napkins, tablecloths, and paper plates and cups. They should be encouraged to keep the theme English. Flowers are a must! The paper plates (use the small size), cups, and napkins should have a flower pattern. (If you would prefer to use real teacups, buy some mismatched ones from a local thrift store. These can then be used year after year.)

- **Servers**—The group of students who will be acting as the servers should practice ahead of time. They will be serving the guests on their right sides. They also need to practice saying (in English accents), "Yes, my lord" or "Yes, my lady." All of the servers should wear black and white. The males should wear black ties, and the females should wear white aprons.

- **Music/Entertainment Committee**—This committee will plan and bring English music to play during the tea. They may wish to perform a short skit or drama using English accents. They may also wish to make an oral presentation about the things that they learned about during this unit.

The entire class (besides the servers) should dress appropriately for an English tea. The boys may choose to wear ties, suits, hats, etc. The girls may choose to wear long dresses, shawls, gloves, hats, etc.

To help your students further understand English ways and English mansions, rent for your students a video which is set in England (preferably in the 1950s or 1960s). Be sure to preview the movie before showing it to your class. Play the entire movie or sections of it to show the formality, manners, division in classes, and the countryside.

On the following pages are some instructions for the tea and some recipes for the food. You may wish to prepare the recipes yourself, create them at school and have them cooked by a school cook, or ask some parent volunteers to prepare them at home. Whatever you decide to do, be certain that it is in accordance with the rules of your school district.

Classroom Teatime *(cont.)*

Manners

Before the tea takes place, discuss proper English tea manners with the students. Below are some guidelines for them. Let the students practice their manners prior to the tea, using empty teacups.

- **Ladies**—A lady holds a teacup in her left or right hand. She sips slowly. A lady's ankles should be crossed during teatime, and her back should be straight. When using a serviette (napkin), she politely dabs her mouth.
- **Gentlemen**—A gentleman should help seat the ladies and push in their chairs courteously. A gentleman should always sit with a straight back and wipe his mouth with a serviette (napkin).

Recipes

Dropped Scones

Ingredients

- 8 ounces (240 mL) flour
- ¼ teaspoon (1.25 mL) salt
- 1 oz. (30 mL) shortening
- 1 tablespoon (15 mL) powdered sugar
- 1 teaspoon (5 mL) baking powder
- 2–3 teaspoons (10–15 mL) sour milk
- 1 egg

Directions

1. Mix together all of the dry ingredients thoroughly.
2. Blend in the shortening.
3. Beat in the egg and then add the milk until the mixture becomes soft. Beat well.
4. Heat a pan, and spray it with cooking oil.
5. Drop a spoonful of dough on the hot surface.
6. Cook the dough until it is brown underneath and bubbly on top and then turn it over and brown the other side.
7. Cool slightly and then spread it with butter and jam. Grease the pan between each scone.

Nut and Cherry Tea Bread

Ingredients

- 12 ounces (360 mL) self-rising flour
- ½ teaspoon (2.5 mL) salt
- 2 ounces (60 mL) flaked or chopped nuts
- ½ pint (240 mL) milk
- 1 large egg
- 3 ounces (80 mL) halved glacé cherries
- 2 ounces (60 mL) melted butter/margarine
- 3 ounces (80 mL) castor sugar (powdered)

Directions

1. Mix the flour, salt, and sugar.
2. Save a few cherries and nuts for the cake top. Mix the rest into the flour mixture.
3. Beat the milk and egg to stiffness. Stir in melted butter/margarine.
4. Pour the mixture into a loaf pan.
5. Arrange the nuts and cherries on the top.
6. Bake at 350°F (180°C) for 1 to 1 ¼ hours. Let the bread cool. Serve it sliced and buttered.

Classroom Teatime *(cont.)*

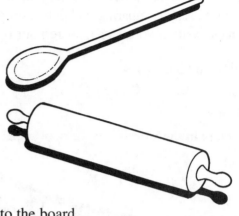

Shortbread Biscuits (Cookies)

Ingredients
- 6 ounces (180 mL) of plain flour
- 1 ½ cups (360 mL) ground rice
- 5 ounces (140 g) margarine or butter
- powdered sugar
- flour (to sprinkle on board))

Directions
1. Sift the dry ingredients together.
2. Rub in the butter until the mixture is crumbly.
3. Sprinkle a board with flour. Roll the dough out onto the board.
4. Press the dough mixture with your fingers until it becomes like putty. Do not add moisture.
5. Wrap the dough in waxed paper. Place it in the refrigerator until it is cold.
6. Sprinkle the board with flour. Roll the dough out to ¼ inch (.8 cm) thickness on the board.
7. Cut out biscuits with a wavy-edged cutter.
8. Place the biscuits on a greased pan.
9. Bake at 350°F (180°C) for 15 to 20 minutes.
10. Sprinkle with powdered sugar.

Basic Bun Mixture

Ingredients
- 8 ounces (240 mL) flour
- 4 ounces (120 mL) powdered sugar
- 4 ounces (112 g) butter or margarine
- 2 tablespoons (30 mL) milk
- 1 ½ teaspoons (8 mL) baking powder

Directions
1. Sift the flour and salt in a basin.
2. Stir in the margarine until the mixture is crumbly.
3. Add the sugar and baking powder.
4. Mix in the egg and milk until the mixture is stiff enough for a fork to stand upright.
5. Using two forks, place the mixture in small, rocky heaps on a greased baking sheet. Space them apart.
6. Bake in an oven at 425°F (220°C) for 12 to 15 minutes (until lightly browned).

Variations *Coconut buns*—Add 2–3 ounces (60–80 mL) of shredded coconut. *Lemon buns*—Add the juice and grated rind of half of a lemon. Add less milk. *Raspberry buns*—Flatten the heaps slightly, and make a hollow well inside each one. Fill the wells with jam and then pull the dough up and around the jam so that it is sealed inside. Sprinkle with powdered sugar.

Compare and Contrast

View the recently released movie *The Borrowers*. Look over the topics below and keep them in mind as you watch the movie. After you have watched it, choose one or two of the topics and write a 100 (or more) word essay comparing and contrasting the movie to the original story of *The Borrowers*. After you have written your essay, share your opinions and findings with the class.

- clothing and hairstyles
- speech
- story plot
- characters in the story
- setting

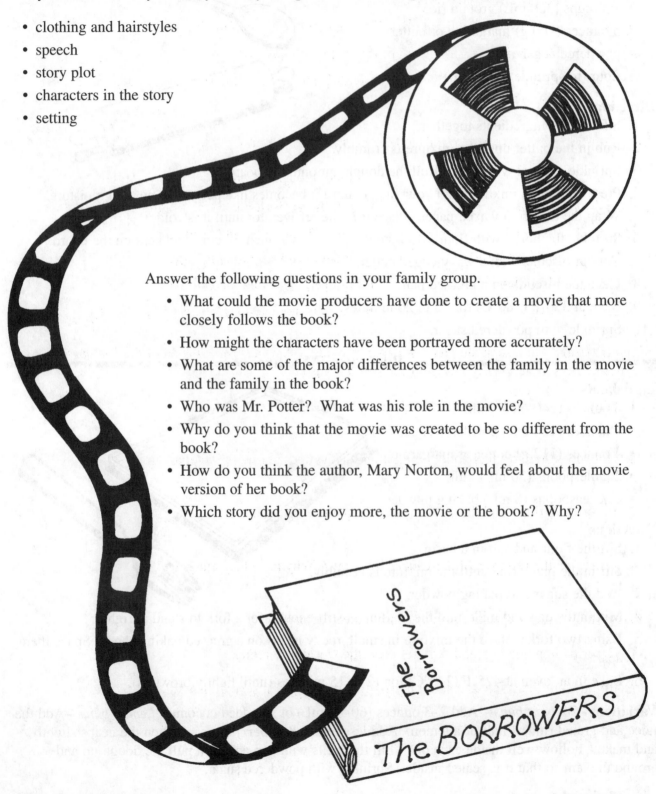

Answer the following questions in your family group.

- What could the movie producers have done to create a movie that more closely follows the book?
- How might the characters have been portrayed more accurately?
- What are some of the major differences between the family in the movie and the family in the book?
- Who was Mr. Potter? What was his role in the movie?
- Why do you think that the movie was created to be so different from the book?
- How do you think the author, Mary Norton, would feel about the movie version of her book?
- Which story did you enjoy more, the movie or the book? Why?

Unit Test

True or False: Write true or false next to each statement.

1._____The Clock family is the only family of Borrowers still in the mansion.

2._____Pod is a very good Borrower.

3._____The boy was sent from Brazil to England because of his illness.

4._____Mrs. Driver is very aware of things in the household.

5._____At one point in the book, Mrs. Driver and Mr. Crampfurl are convinced that the boy has a pet parrot.

Matching: Match the names of the characters to the qualities which identify them.

1._____Pod   A. kind, thoughtful, lonely

2._____Homily   B. old, loves stories, believes in miniature people

3._____the boy   C. very selfish, loves pretty things

4._____Mr. Crampfurl   D. great borrower, growing older

5._____Mrs. May   E. thinker, observant, patient, odd

6._____Arrietty   F. curious, not cautious, wants friends, lonely

Short Answer: On a separate piece of paper, provide a short answer for each of the following questions. Be sure to clearly number each of your answers.

1. Why do Pod and Homily protect Arrietty so much?

2. How does Arrietty feel about emigrating? How does her mother feel about it?

3. How are Arrietty and the boy similar? Name two differences.

4. Where do the relatives of the Clocks live now? Why have they emigrated?

Essay: Answer these questions on a separate piece of paper.

1. Describe how the boy and Arrietty view the world differently.

2. If you were to awake as a small person one morning, list several benefits and several disadvantages you would experience.

Responses

Directions: Explain the meaning of each of these quotations from *The Borrowers*.

Chapter 2: *Do you realize . . . that your poor father risks his life every time he borrows a potato?*

Chapter 4: *To go and live like Hendreary and Lupy in a badger's set! The other side of the world, that's where they say it is—all among the earthworms.*

Chapter 6: *Upstairs is a dangerous place, said Pod.*

Chapter 8: *. . . but never climb down anything that isn't fixed like. Supposing one of them came along and moved the shoescraper—where would you be then?*

Chapter 9: *. . . if someone could hold them, and turn the pages. I'm not a bit bilingual. I can read anything.*

Chapter 12: *Three days running he's looked and nothing there. He'll give up hope now . . . he'll never look again.*

Chapter 14: *. . . please understand! I'm trying to save the race!*

Chapter 16: *. . . pry and potter all you want—two can play at that game!*

Chapter 17: *. . . little people like with hands—or mice dressed up.*

Chapter 19: *And Great-Aunt Sophy had the same suspicion: she was furious when she heard that Mrs. Driver had seen several little people when she herself on a full decanter had only risen to one or, at most, two. Crampfurl had to bring all the Madeira up from the cellar and stack the cases against the wall in a corner of Aunt Sophy's bedroom where, as she said, she could keep an eye on it.*

Note to the Teacher: Choose an appropriate number of quotes for your students.

Conversations

Directions: Work with a partner to perform the conversations that might have occurred in each of the following situations.

- Mrs. May and the little girl when she first hears about the Borrowers

- Pod and Arrietty when they go on Arrietty's first borrowing experience

- Pod and Homily when they discuss emigrating and Eggletina

- Arrietty and the boy in the outside world

- The views of Homily and Arrietty on emigrating

- Mr. Crampfurl and Mrs. Driver when things start disappearing

- Mrs. Driver and the policeman after she sees the Borrowers

- Mrs. Driver and Mr. Crampfurl after their discovery underneath the floorboards

- Mrs. May and her brother as children growing up

- The boy and Mr. Crampfurl as they are outside and the boy is racing around the fields

- The boy and Mrs. Driver after the discovery underneath the floorboards

- The boy and Aunt Sophy, as if he had escaped during his three-day imprisonment

- Aunt Sophy and Mrs. Driver after Mrs. Driver sees the small family

Perform one of your own conversation ideas for the characters in *The Borrowers*. Write your conversation ideas on the lines below

_____

_____

_____

_____

_____

_____

_____

Bibliography

Related Books/Articles

Ardley, Brigette and Neil. *India.* (Silver Burdett Press, 1989)

Arnosky, Jim. *Crinkleroot's Book of Animal Tracking.* (Simon & Schuster Children's, 1990)

De Angeli, Marguerite. *A Door in the Wall: Story of Medieval London.* (Dell, 1990)

Greene, Carol. *England* (Children's Press, 1993)

Langley, Andrew. *Passport to Great Britain.* (Franklin Watts, 1994)

National Geographic. *The Vanishing Prairie Dog.* (April 1998)

Other Books by Mary Norton

Are All the Giants Dead? (Harcourt Brace, 1997)

Bed-Knob and Broomstick.
(Harcourt Brace, 1990)

The Borrowers Afield. (Harcourt Brace, 1998)

The Borrowers Afloat. (Harcourt Brace, 1998)

The Borrowers Aloft. (Harcourt Brace, 1990)

The Borrowers Avenged. (Harcourt Brace, 1990)

The Complete Adventures of the Borrowers.
(Harcourt Brace, 1999)

46

Answer Key

Page 11

1. They kept each other company, and Mrs. May taught Kate many things.
2. It's a story about Borrowers.
3. Her brother told her. He was sent to the house from India to recover from rheumatic fever.
4. Answers will vary. Wallpaper made of discarded writing paper, stamps for wall hangings, etc., can be found.
5. She loved to write in her diary. She did not want to run out of paper.
6. Borrowing is his job. She wants to learn how to borrow.
7. She wants a teacup. He is getting older and it is becoming more difficult for him to climb.
8. Answers will vary. Pod is the father, caring, concerned about Arrietty, and very good at borrowing. Homily is selfish, over-protective, overly tidy. Arrietty is intelligent, can read and write, and is usually obedient and curious.
9. He is seen. They must emigrate, and Arrietty must learn about Eggletina.
10. She will not give up her possessions.

Page 16

1. Answers will vary.
2. She selfishly sent him. They might be killed or caught.
3. Pod is the best at borrowing.
4. The boy sees him. He helps Pod carry the cup to the bottom of the curtain.
5. They wake her to tell her about Aunt Lupy, Uncle Hendreary, Eggletina, and the upstairs.
6. Answers will vary. She feels confined, restricted, and lonely. She wants to know what is outside, she mouths off about emigrating, and she is excited about going outside.
7. She likes the idea. She can learn to take care of herself.
8. Answers will vary.

9. She wants to go borrowing with her father. She swept and trod the passageways, sorted and graded the beads into bottles, cut kids gloves into squares, filed fish-bone needles, and hung up the wash.
10. She is very distracted, overwhelmed, and excited. Pod lets her go out on the lawn.

Page 21

1. Answers will vary.
2. She goes to the grate. Homily would like some blotting paper.
3. She meets the boy.
4. She has a very narrow idea of how large the world is, and she feels that humans exist for the sake of the Borrowers.
5. He swam around and fished things out.
6. She feels that they only need a few humans for their own survival and to keep up their standard of living.
7. She thinks Pod comes out of the wine decanter and that he is a part of her imagination.
8. She is very strict, and she makes him do his schoolwork.
9. The humans are dying out. The boy says the humans are everywhere and the little people are dying out.
10. She writes a letter to her cousins and goes to see the boy in his room.

Page 22

Now that I am small, how different the world looks!

Page 23

Meet me outside the classroom by the tree at noon.

Page 24

bobby—policeman	windscreen—windshield
bonnet—car hood	petrol—gasoline
boot—car trunk	crisps—potato chips
chips—french fries	cooker—stove
draughts—checkers	fortnight—two weeks
lift—elevator	cheers—thank you,
motorway—freeway	good-bye
jumper—sweater	loo—toilet
ta—thanks	

Answer Key (cont.)

Page 26
1. Answers will vary.
2. She is worried about being the last Borrower alive. She is going to the storeroom.
3. She goes to the boy's room.
4. She had to go because her father called for her. The boy understands this.
5. The boy gives Arrietty a message from her Uncle Hendreary.
6. He asks her to tell Aunt Lupy to return home.
7. He takes her downstairs and makes her tell him what is going on.
8. They are concerned about Arrietty's life and safety. He does not trust them; he only borrows from them.
9. The boy opens the roof to their house to give them gifts.
10. He gives them furniture and other household items. Pod has to rearrange their household over and over.

Page 29
1. 7
2. 5032
3. 1717
4. 177
5. 88
6. 73
7. 209
8. 7654
9. 2967
10. 178

Page 31
1. Answers will vary.
2. They have become less concerned, almost careless, about being seen. Homily has become very materialistic, and Arrietty has gained a friend.
3. Mrs. Driver starts to notice that things are missing.
4. They love the wealth but feel sad because they have no one to invite over.
5. Arrietty is now allowed to be friends with the boy.
6. She finds the home of the Clock family. She thinks she saw mice dressed up in clothing.

7. He tells them to get in the laundry bag, and he will take them to safety. Mrs. Driver locks the boy up for three days.
8. He explains that little people called Borrowers merely borrowed the items to survive.
9. The police and an exterminator are called in.
10. Mrs. May has Arrietty's writing book.

Page 34
1. 9,192,090
2. 100,691
3. 340,435
4. 60,804
5. 79,617
6. 767,696
7. 2,697,214
8. 873,668,101
9. 813,008
10. 467,222

Page 43
True or False
1. True
2. True
3. False
4. True
5. False

Matching
1. D
2. C
3. A
4. E
5. B
6. F

Short Answer
1. They love her and are concerned for her safety.
2. Arrietty wants to emigrate. Her mother does not.
3. Answers will vary.
4. They have emigrated to nearby fields. They emigrated because they were seen, and therefore, they feared for their safety.

Essay:
1. Answers will vary.
2. Answers will vary.

Page 44
Answers will vary.

Page 45
Answers will vary.